**Cover:**
Foote Bros, 1945
**Front endpapers:**
American Airlines, 1944
Pan American Airlines, 1957
**Back endpapers:**
The Airlines of the United States, 1945
American Airlines, 1944

© 2002 TASCHEN GmbH
Hohenzollernring 53, D–50672 Köln
**www.taschen.com**

Editor: Jim Heiman, L.A.
Design: Claudia Frey, Cologne
Production: Tina Ciborowius, Cologne

Printed in Italy
ISBN 3–8228–1626–4

# SEE THE
# WORLD

**TASCHEN**

KÖLN LONDON MADRID NEW YORK PARIS TOKYO

ARRIVE IN CAL

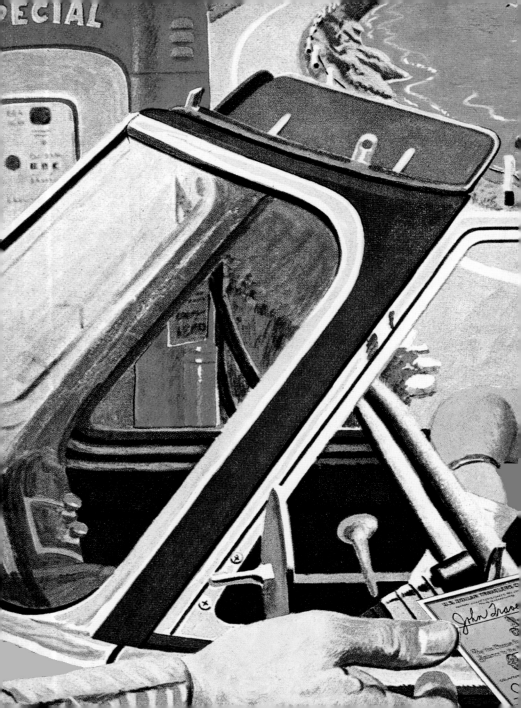

# California

The glamorous Golden State . . . bordered by the blue Pacific. From dawn to dusk, always something to see and do.

# Pacific Northwest

Noted for its mountains, sparkling waters, forests and flowers. Union Pacific parallels the Columbia River Gorge for 200 miles.

# Sun Valley
### IDAHO

Year-'round vacation playground. Swimming in glass-walled pools . . . skating on an artificial ice-rink. Golfing and other sports.

## Utah · Arizona
### NATIONAL PARKS

Grouped in one vast scenic area are Southern Utah's Bryce Canyon and Zion National Parks . . . Arizona's Grand Canyon National Park.

## Colorado

Mile-high summer playgrounds with a delightful, cool climate that brings relief from summer's heat.

## Dude Ranches

Throughout the "Union Pacific West" are scores of dude ranches offering a variety of outdoor activities and a choice of accommodations:

*Union Pacific Railroad, 1949*

# Anytime is a good time to visit MEXICO.

For change, rest and recreation, board an American Airlines Flagship for Mexico. In a few hours you can be in a vivid, exciting land of enchanting variety. Telephone your nearest American Airlines ticket office for complete information.

American Airlines directly serves the major industrial cities in the United States. Along our routes, also, are America's famous vacation-lands from Southern California and Sun Country of the southwest to the year-round attractions of New England.

Monterrey

Mexico City

A traveler's paradise—friendly, colorful and fascinating. The floating gardens at Xochimilco attract tourists from all over the world. You will be welcomed with kindness and courtesy. It is frequently said that Americans "become more mellow" in Mexico.

Fishermen at Lake Patzcuaro with old butterfly-type fishing nets. Traveling through Mexico reveals an almost endless panorama of native costumes, customs and charms . . . all within easy reach from any airline port in the States. Going by Flagship allows a longer visit.

## AMERICAN AIRLINES *System*
### THE NATIONAL AND INTERNATIONAL ROUTE OF THE FLAGSHIPS

The land of ancient Aztecs, who weaved humming bird feathers into cloth, erected pyramids similar to those in Egypt and read the stars "with almost Greenwich precision." Also the land of modern art, grand opera, and an increasingly-important international capital.

Mexico is different—a unique blend of the old world in villages, and the new world of modern conveniences and entertainment in its cities. Its resorts, such as Acapulco, offer bathing and deep sea fishing. Ask your nearest American Airlines office or your travel agent.

*John Fisher*

Fairyland in Stone! Carlsbad Caverns National Park is one of the world's great natural wonders. It dwarfs all other caverns in size—contains 2¾ miles of lighted paths. Its formations are the most spectacular of all. Your entire family will be thrilled. Easy conducted tours. Three elevators for your convenience.

# EXCITING AS A FOREIGN LAND! COMFORTABLE AS HOME!

*Come enjoy a really different vacation this summer in high, cool New Mexico!*

Mission Church, Isleta Pueblo. New Mexico's many interesting landmarks are closer than you think. Wherever you live in the U.S., you can drive here, tour state and return home, all within 2 weeks.

See Navaho Indians driving wagons on side roads near the main highways. Visit pueblos and reservations. Watch Indians make pottery—bake bread in outdoor ovens.

Sightseeing is fun here! New Mexico's 7000 miles of paved highways lead you to modern cities, national monuments, state parks and vast national forests.

Quaint shops, galleries, museums and distinctive architecture give Santa Fe a continental flavor.

Aztec Ruins—remnants of a culture that thrived long before Columbus discovered America.

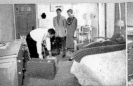

Hospitality Plus! You'll find good lodgings in New Mexico's more than 1600 hotels, motels, resorts and ranches. Fine restaurants here, too.

Elephant Butte Lake, tops for bass fishing. Northern lakes and streams offer trout. Excellent hunting and skiing in season.

Ride, camp, picnic in New Mexico's 8½ million acres of national forests. Days are clear, sunny. Nights cool, starlit.

# NEW MEXICO

LAND OF ENCHANTMENT

**FREE** BOOKLETS AND MAPS! Write New Mexico State Tourist Bureau, Box 5530-B, Santa Fe, New Mexico

North Carolina, 1951

*Visit Colorful*

# NORTH CAROLINA

*American Airlines, 1950*

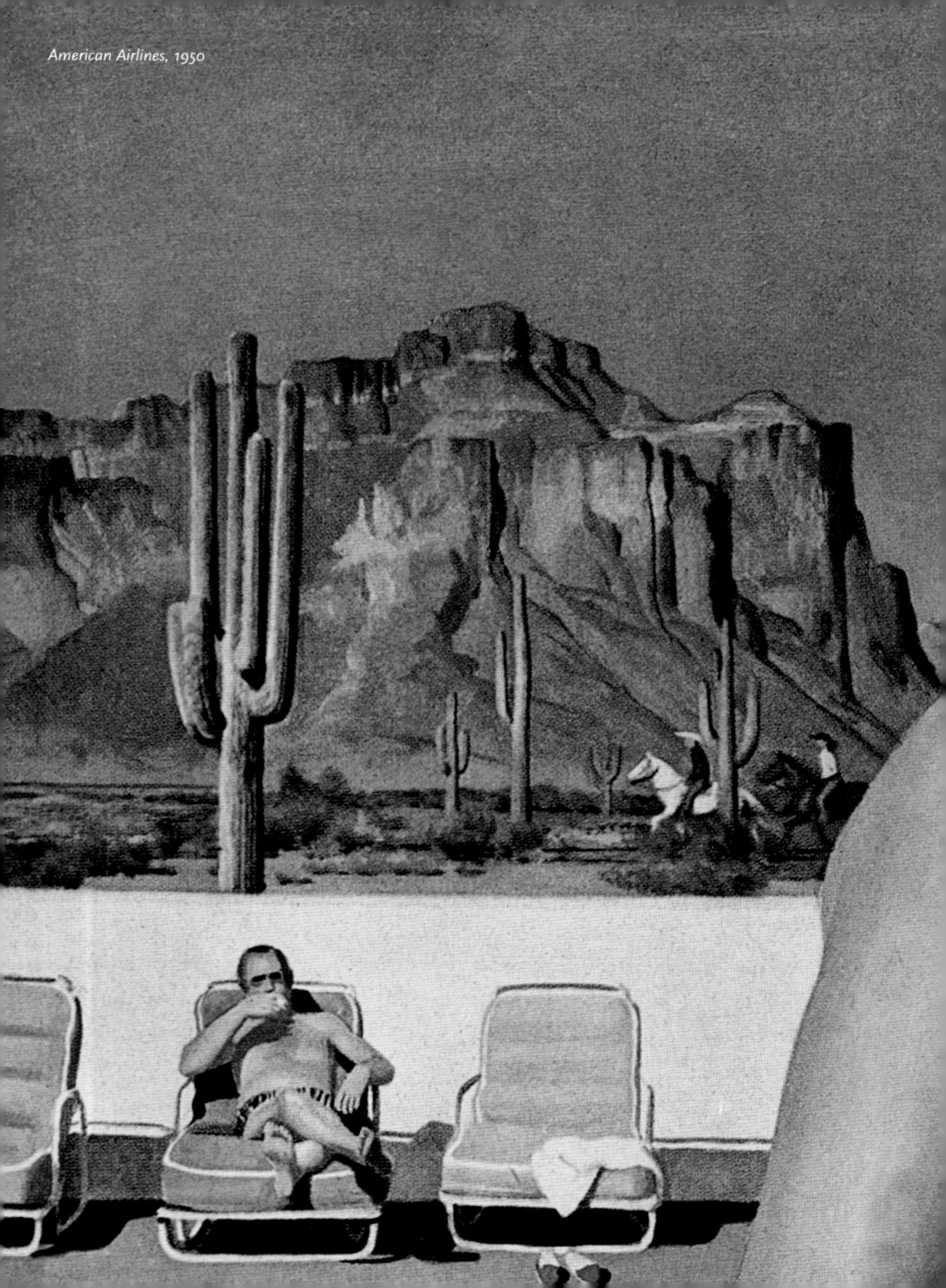

# DO YOU KNOW <u>FALL</u> IN

## *Southern California*

**ALL THAT'S DELIGHTFUL** in Southern California's summer lasts right on through September and October...bright, warm days ...cool nights...with little or no rain.

That's why, especially in this unsettled year, the experienced traveler avoids the "peak" season and plans a vacation when transportation and accommodations are more readily available. Of course, *it is essential to have confirmed accommodations in advance*...and the later you can come the easier it will be to get reservations.

So try the fall. You'll find everything as exciting as always... Pacific beaches, high mountains, gay foreign quarters, movieland night spots...in fact, all the wonders for which Los Angeles County and entire Southern California are famous.

**Dance** to the music of name bands at smart supper clubs...join celebrities at world premieres, movie previews, transcontinental broadcasts...visit unique theaters...dine in quaint Chinese, Russian and Italian restaurants. Stand on a mountaintop, the lights of sixty cities twinkling below.

**Explore** near-by mountains...flower-filled fields...mountain streams teeming with trout. Drive to high passes or ride to higher peaks for unforgettable panoramas. Go motorboating on a mile-high lake...or bathe in a medicinal hot spring. Relax under pines by a glowing campfire.

**Bask** on broad, Pacific beaches...surfboard on long, rolling breakers. Troll for big-game fish...sail in a regatta or off to a romantic pleasure isle to see exotic birds, strange plants and flowers.

ALL-YEAR CLUB OF SOUTHERN CALIFORNIA, LTD.

*This advertisement sponsored by the Los Angeles County Board of Supervisors for the citizens of Beverly Hills, Glendale, Hollywood, Long Beach, Los Angeles, Pasadena, Pomona, Santa Monica and 152 other communities. Copyright, 1946, by All-Year Club of Southern California, Ltd.—a non-profit community organization serving vacationists.*

### *Southern California*

If you find you must wait for accommodations, just remember: nothing else can ever take the place of this vacation of a lifetime...it <u>is</u> worth waiting for.

**Golf** on palm-bordered fairways, where champions compete. Join the crowds at world-famous horse races...rodeos, fiestas. Discover fragrant orange groves...ancient wineries...new, unusual industries...celebrated shops showing California's latest style creations.

# Southern California

**Golden Crown DC-7's - Fastest to**

*Miami Beach*

**and the Caribbean**

# Acapulco

WESTWARD, the Mediterranean's fabulous "Côte d'Azur" has moved across the world. Yachtsmen of the sophisticated set now drop anchor in the azure waters of the Mexican Riviera, with alluring Acapulco their favorite port of call. Sheer heights of volcanic mountains rise abruptly from the sparkling Pacific. Terraced palaces contrast the picturesque countryside, unchanged since the days of the Spanish Conquistadors. Your CORSAIR Cruise, aboard the finest cruise ship afloat, takes you to Old Mexico, land of intriguing color. Your days will be as full as you want to make them: Lazy hours on the white sands of Acapulco's famed beach, a dip into the invigorating rollers of the Pacific; a try at deep-sea fishing; the thrill of traditional bull fights; a round of seeing foreign sights; luxurious rest in an ultra-modern hotel; dancing in smart night spots . . . with always, the haunting romance of Latin music under a tropical moon. The CORSAIR sails direct from Long Beach, California, to Acapulco, Mexico, every 12 days. **Consult Your Travel Agent for Rates and Particulars.**

*The CORSAIR! Built by the late J. Pierpont Morgan for his personal use in cruising the oceans of the world, expense was no object in her construction and fittings. When the vessel was launched, no ship as luxurious had ever been afloat. Now her interior has been completely restored, and once again the CORSAIR takes her rightful place as the finest cruise ship on any sea.*

PACIFIC LINES CRUISES

SKINNER BUILDING • SEATTLE 1, WASHINGTON

Where a Vacation
is an Adventure

Pueblo
Eagle Dancer

*New York State, 1953*

WHEN THE
WAR CLOUDS
ROLL AWAY·

A JOY·FULL WORLD

White Motor Co., 1946

Boeing, 1946

McDonnell Aircraft Corporation, 1945

*United Airlines, 1946*

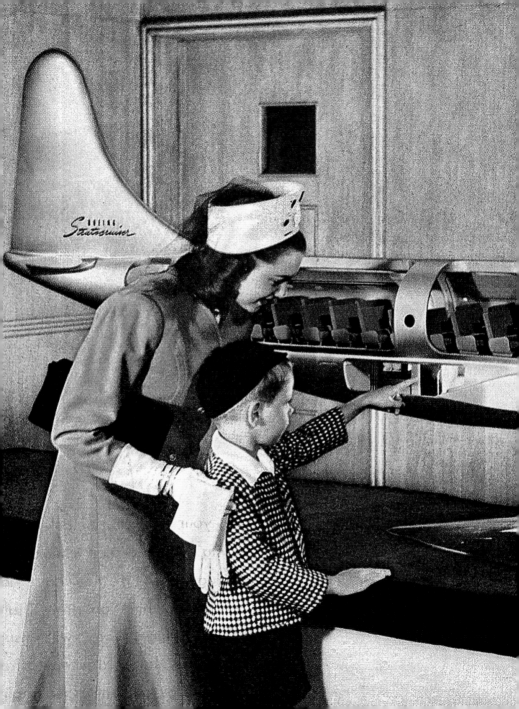

*Boeing, 1946*

*The Airlines of the United States, 1945*

# the New World

*Lockheed, 1941*

NAPIER UNIVERSITY LIS

ALL FIRST CLASS MAIL by AIR

IT'S COMING!

CHICAGO AND SOUTH
COLONIAL AIR
CONTINENTAL A
DELTA AIR
EASTERN AIR
INLAND AIR
MID-CONTINENT
NATIONAL AIR
NORTHEAST AI
NORTHWEST A
PAN AMERICAN A
PAN AMERICAN-GRAC
PENNSYLVANIA-CENTR
TRANSCONTINENTAL &
UNITED AIR L
WESTERN AIR

The Airlines of the United States, 1945

Piper, 1946

Piper, 1946

*Lockheed, 1940*

TWA, 1946

*Foote Bros, 1945*

*TWA, 1946*

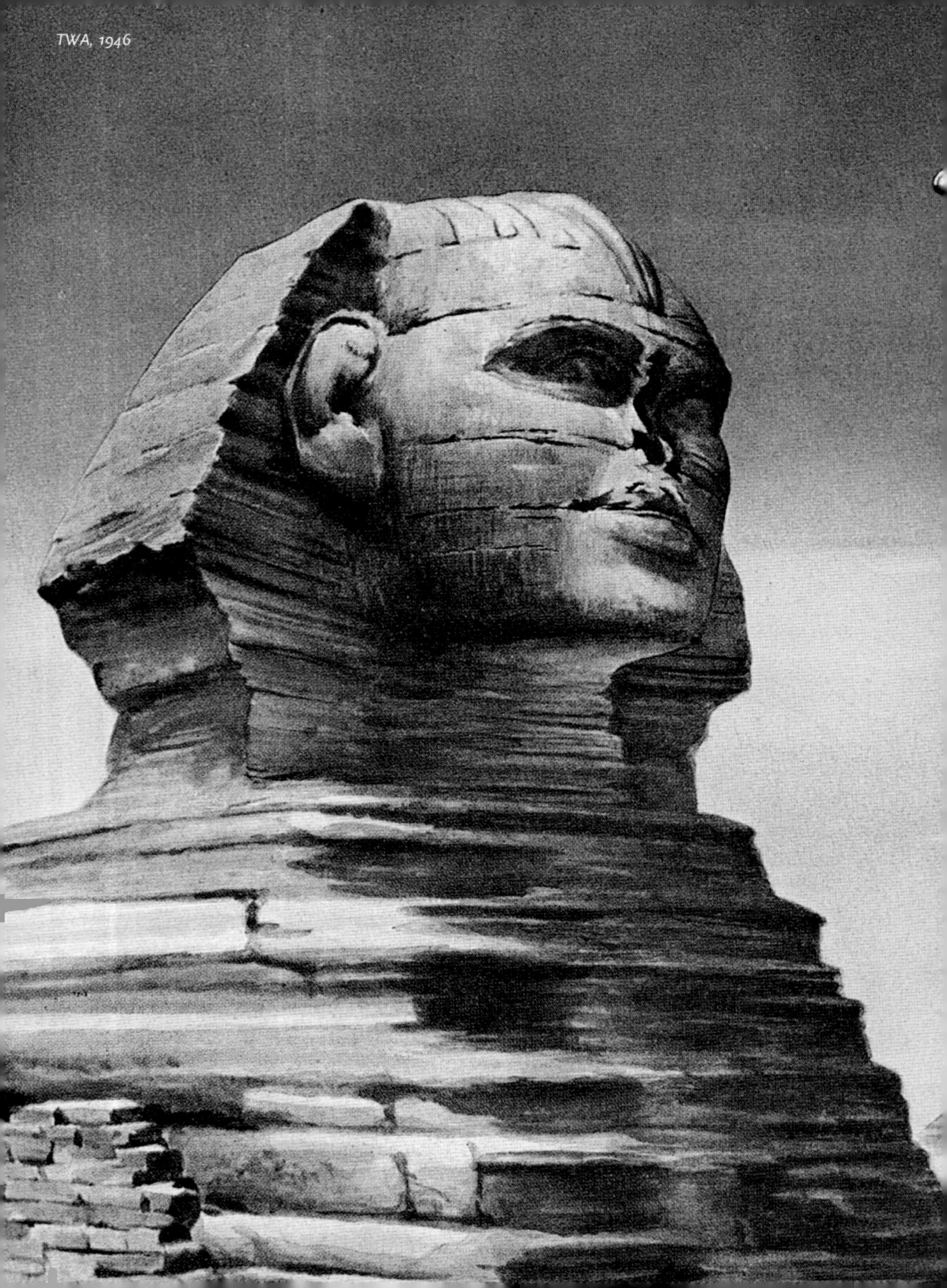

TWA, 1946

TWA, 1946

American Airlines, 1950

*American Airlines, 1951*

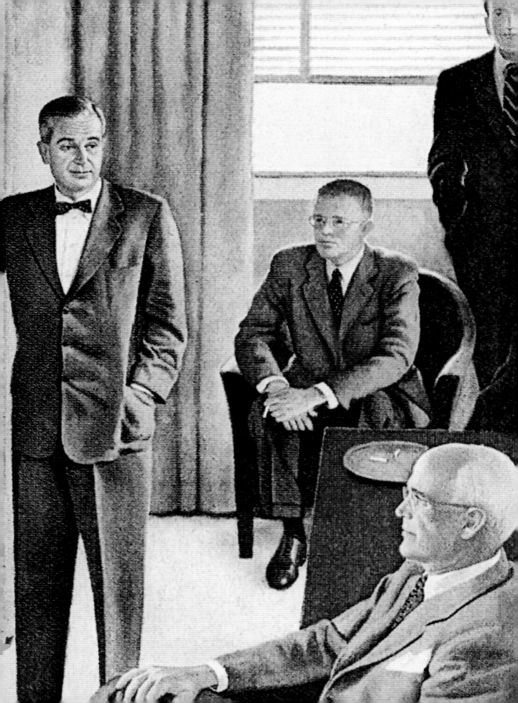

Boeing, 1959

Borg-Warner, 1954

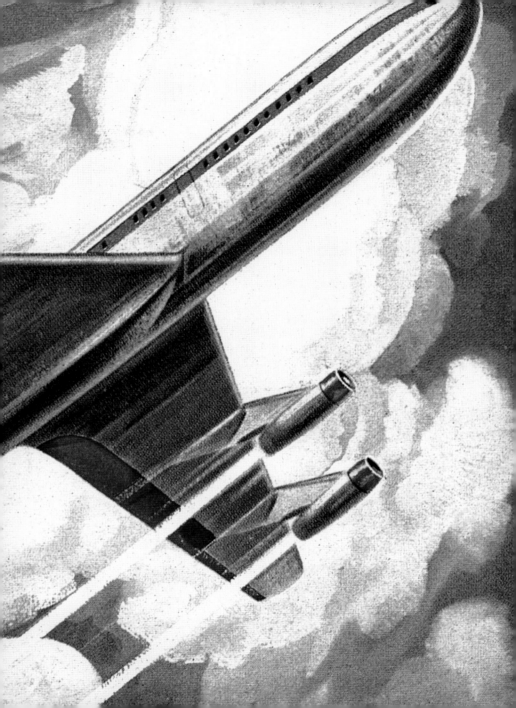

UNITED A

*United Air Lines, 1952*

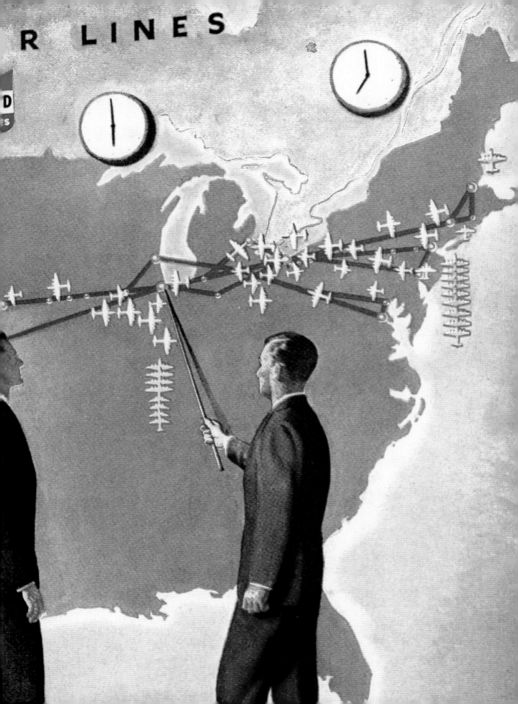

Martin Aircraft, 1945

Now...An
the Shor
Between

American Airlines, 1946

# What airline gives you Red Carpet*Service?

It's "Red Carpet" luxury all the way...

aboard United's special nonstop DC-7s!

Inviting lounge, superlative service...

de luxe meals and refreshments!

Games, kits, scores of travel items...

many other "extras" at no extra cost!

United Air Lines, 1956

BOAC, 1959

*Pan American Air Lines, 1959*

TWA, 1951

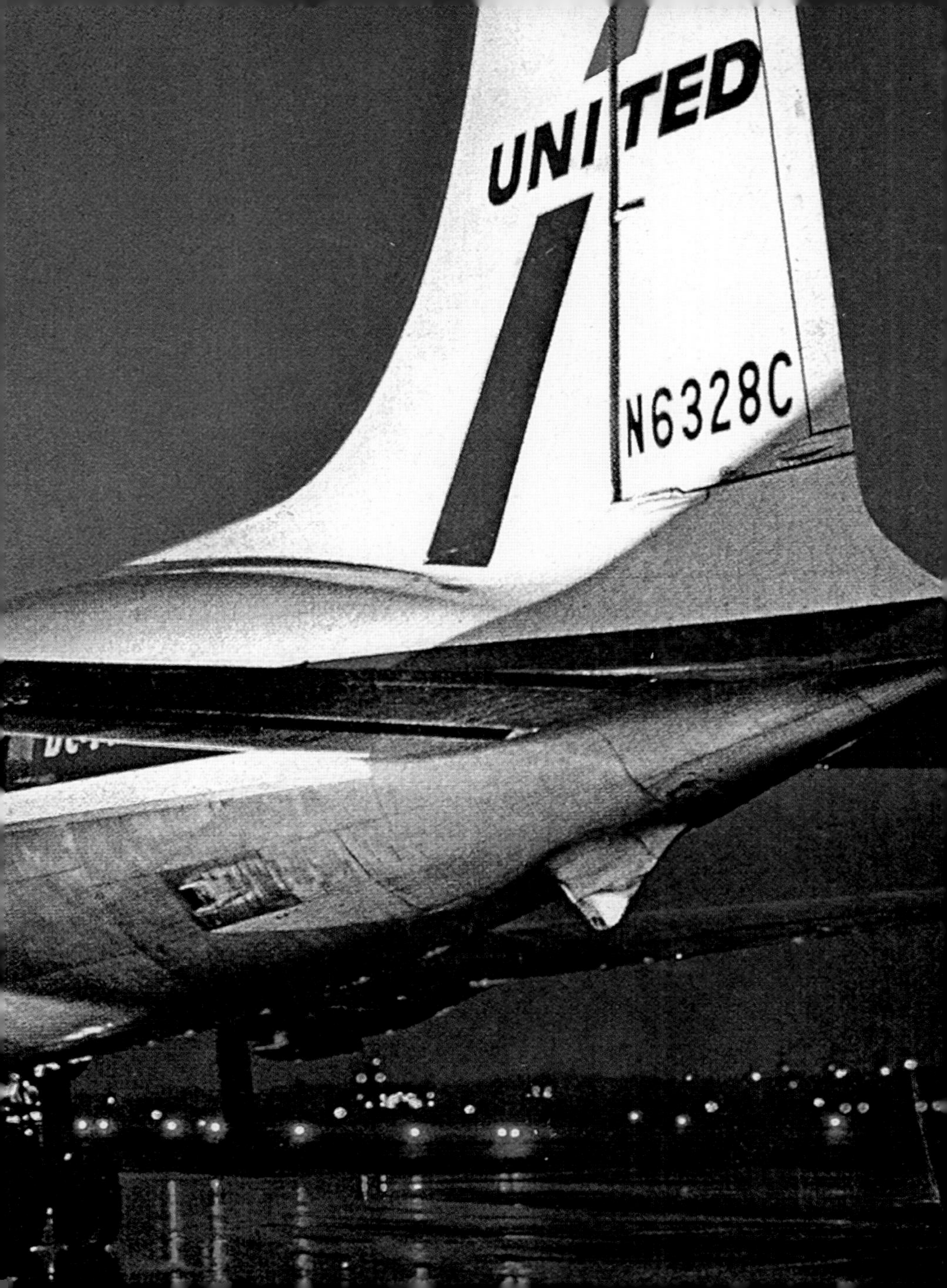
UNITED
N6328C

a. Leydenfrost

*Douglas Aircraft, 1953*

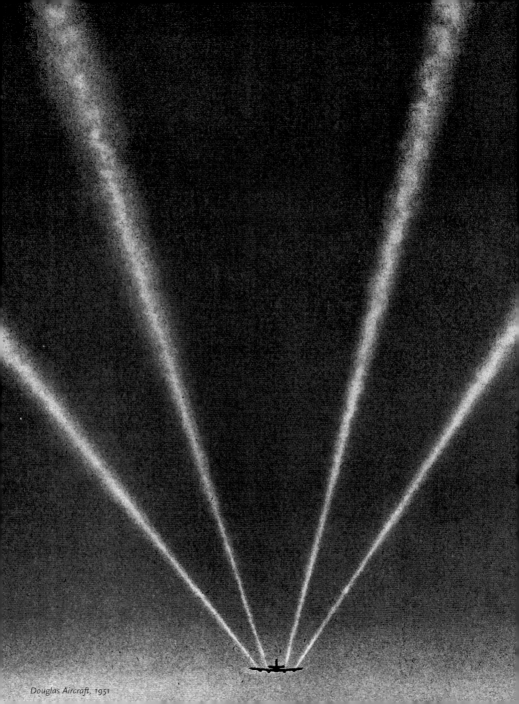

Douglas Aircraft, 1951

# For the SWORDS of today...

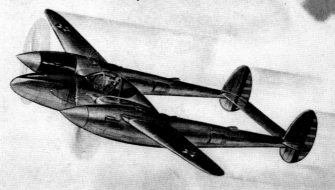

## and the PLOWSHARES of tomorrow...

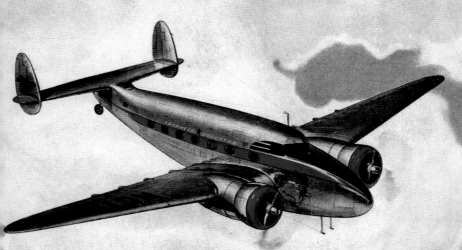

The swords of 1941 are fast and deadly fighting airplanes. Their blades are the whirling, powerful propellers that rocket them through the air at unprecedented speeds in defense of nations.

In building these airplanes Lockheed is doing a patriotic duty. But hopefully, Lockheed looks to the day when these blades will cleave new paths to commerce, peace and expanded industry.

# LOOK TO *Lockheed* FOR LEADERSHIP IN BOTH

LOCKHEED AIRCRAFT CORPORATION · BURBANK, CALIF.

ALL FIRST CLASS MAIL by AIR · IT'S COMING!

*Lockheed, 1941*

Goodyear Aircraft Corporation, 1940

Lockheed, 1951

*United Air Lines, 1958*

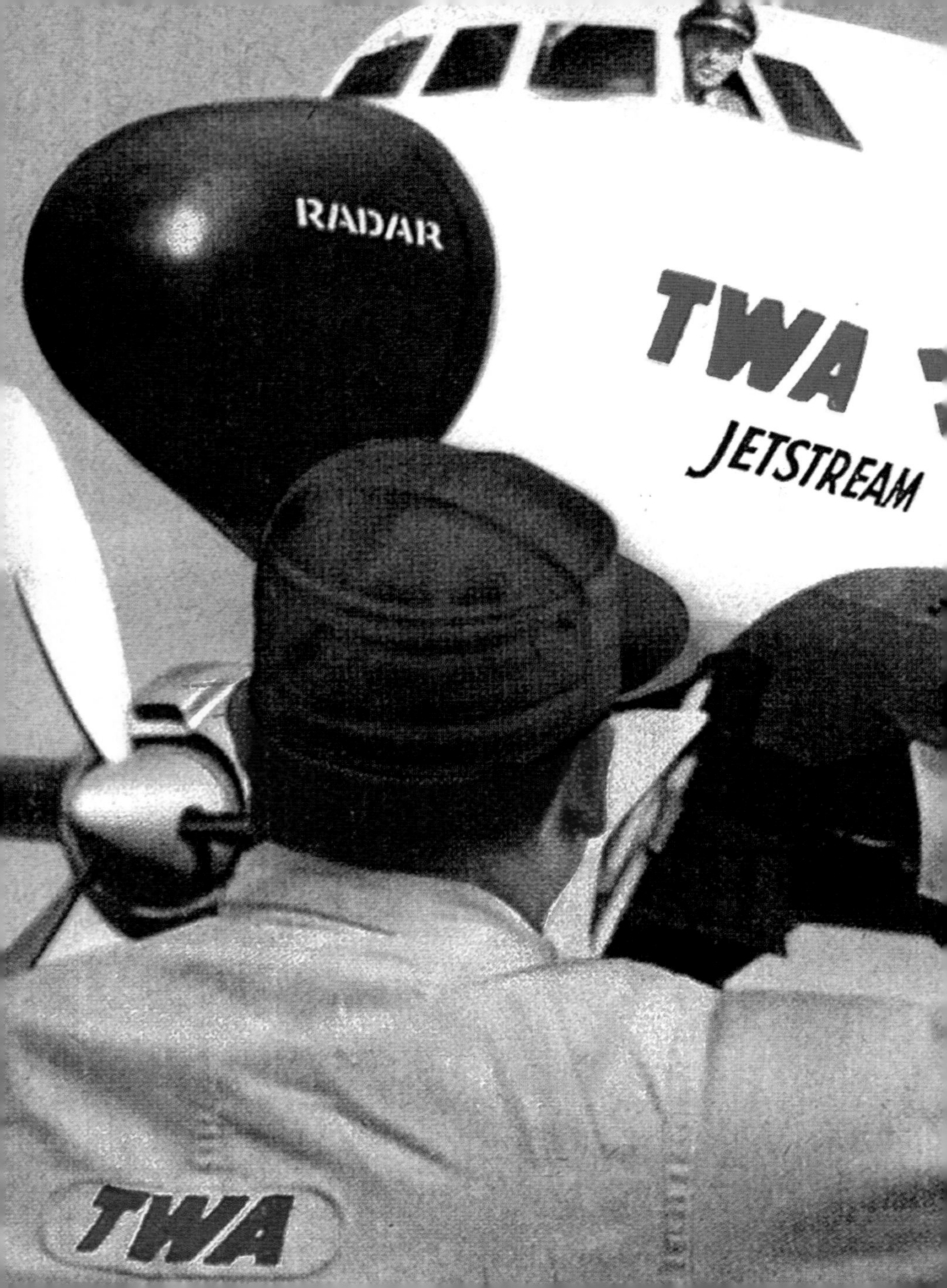
RADAR
TWA
JETSTREAM
TWA

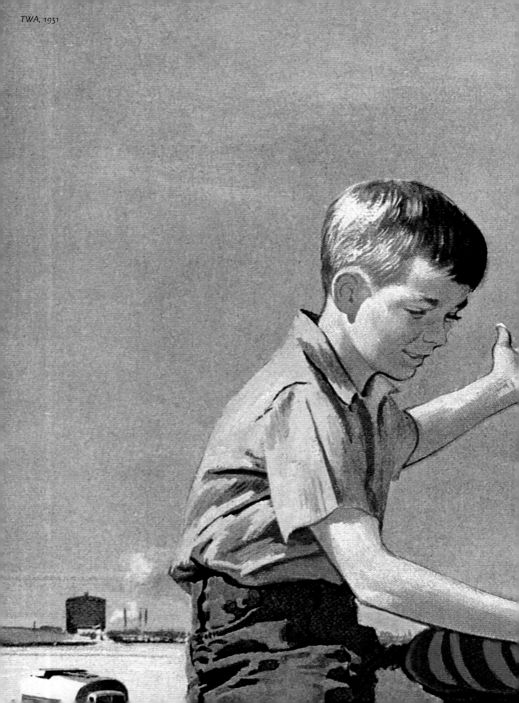

UNITED

O AIR LINES

*United Air Lines, 1952*

© U.A.L. 1952

Laurent
fine

Waikiki Beach, famous symbol
of the Hawaiian Islands

...ountains, one of Canada's
...s and vacation areas

Ed Hall

American Airlines, 1956

*The Commodore*

**19'6" DE LUXE RUNABOUT**

*Gar Wood Industries, 1947*

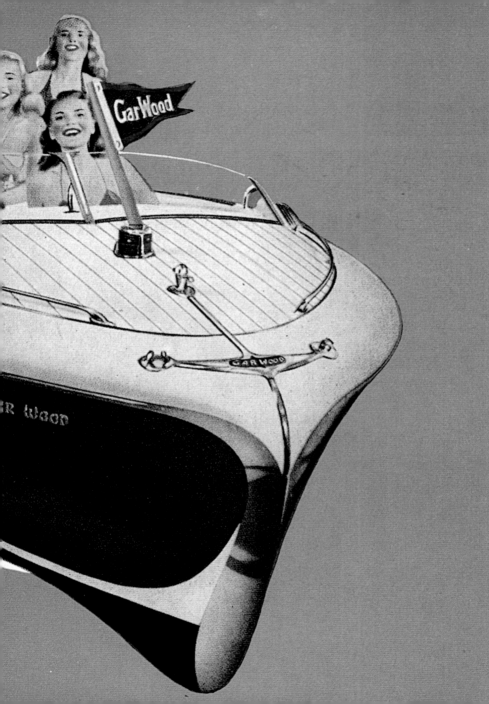

Electric Boat Company, 1945

NEW *Elco* STANDA

*Rew*

*rd of Victory!*

IN BOATING  BORN AND PROVEN IN *Elco* PTs

# Getting there is half the fun!

See your Cunard-authorized Travel Agent and . . .

## GO CUNARD

QUEEN ELIZABETH · QUEEN MARY · MAURETANIA · CARONIA · BRITANNIC · MEDIA · PARTHIA
FRANCONIA · SCYTHIA · SAMARIA · ASCANIA · SAXONIA

An 18" x 22" color reproduction of this painting, without the advertising text and suitable for framing,
will be sent upon request. Write: Cunard Line, 25 Broadway, New York 4, N. Y.

# GETTING THERE IS HALF THE FUN

Crossing to Europe or cruising to faraway places...
*don't miss* the joy of going Cunard! Days and nights
of enchanted relaxation... laughter, music,
sparkling companionship... and the sheer wizardry of master chefs
... make your voyage a brilliant holiday in itself.

*See your Cunard-authorized
travel agent and...* **GO CUNARD**

American Presidents Line, 1948

Fred Lickens

The lovely new *Andrea Doria*

## These men have built a ship...

What gives a ship that thing called personality? From where come those qualities of warmth and friendliness? How do you take the coldness out of steel? How do you breathe life into glass and tile? You won't find the answer in blueprints. You can't do it with money or calloused hands. You build such a ship with your heart.

Into every detail of this lovely vessel have gone the skill and pride of the greatest artisans of Italy. Every mural, every tapestry, every rug and chair...each exquisite bit of glassware and every glowing tile is the work of craftsmen. Yes, a ship is built of many hearts. This is the tradition of Italy. This is the *Andrea Doria*.

The completely air conditioned *Andrea Doria* enters transatlantic service to New York in January. *Special West India Cruise January 30 . . . 17 glorious days*

## *Italian Line*

"ITALIA" — Società di Navigazione — Genova
See your Travel Agent or
**AMERICAN EXPORT LINES (General Agents)**
39 Broadway, New York 6, N. Y.

Alcoa Steamship Co., 1949 ▶ American President Lines, 1951

# Karachi

# AMERICAN PRESIDENT LINES
## GRAND FLEET OF THE PACIFIC AND 'ROUND THE WORLD

*Motor Bus Lines of America, 1945*

**FOR** *First Choice* **o**

.. go earl
go Greyh

*Greyhound, 1942*

Greyhound, 1942

*Greyhound, 1946*

*California Zephyr, 1949*

Budd, 1945

LESLIE
RAGAN

Budd, 1947

# NOW...
## A Complete *RECREATION CAR*

### Especially Designed for Your Pleasure

A diagrammatic painting of Pennsylvania Railroad's new recreation car.

**In daily service on The Jeffersonian, popular all-coach streamliner between New York and St. Louis!**

A dramatic highlight in Pennsylvania Railroad's new equipment program, this colorful new recreation car provides amusement and entertainment for all ages. A luxurious game and reading lounge . . . a children's playroom . . . a sunken buffet lounge . . . miniature movie theatre —pleasure *with variety.* Be among the first to enjoy it! Reserve a seat on *The Jeffersonian* on your next trip!

**SO ROOMY AND RESTFUL**—the new overnight coaches on *The Jeffersonian.* Only 44 seats to the car—and all reclining! You'll like the new lighting, too—fluorescent, 4 times brighter but easy on the eyes. New-type air-conditioning adds still more comfort.

**EXTRA LARGE MODERN WASHROOMS,** one for women, one for men at the end of each coach—handsomely decorated—with 3 glistening washstands and 2 toilet annexes.

**Enjoy these New Features at Low Coach Fares !**

**THE JEFFERSONIAN**

| Westbound | |
|---|---|
| Lv. New York | 6:15 P.M. |
| Lv. Philadelphia | 7:43 P.M. |
| Lv. Washington | 6:20 P.M. |
| Lv. Baltimore | 7:05 P.M. |
| Ar. Harrisburg | 9:42 P.M. |
| Ar. Columbus | 6:46 A.M. |
| Ar. Indianapolis | 8:21 A.M. |
| Ar. St. Louis | 9:27 A.M. |
| | 1:50 P.M. |
| **Eastbound** | |
| Lv. St. Louis | 1:00 P.M. |
| Lv. Indianapolis | 5:07 P.M. |
| Lv. Dayton | 8:13 P.M. |
| Lv. Columbus | 9:35 P.M. |
| Ar. Harrisburg | 6:51 A.M. |
| Ar. Baltimore | 9:23 A.M. |
| Ar. Washington | 10:10 A.M. |
| Ar. Philadelphia | 8:52 A.M. |
| Ar. New York | 10:25 A.M. |

Recreation car facilities available to Baltimore and Washington passengers between Harrisburg and St. Louis.

## PENNSYLVANIA RAILROAD
*Serving the Nation*

General Motors Locomotives, 1947

Pullman-Standard, 1946

Pullman-Standard, 1944

American Locomotive Company, 1946

*Pullman-Standard, 1941*

New York Central, 1947

*Pennsylvania Railroad, 1946*

*Pennsylvania Railroad, 1946*

Olympian Hiawathas, 1947

*Santa Fe, 1957*

**CADILLAC**

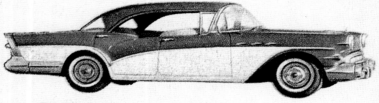

**BUICK**

**OLDSMOBILE**

**CHEVROLET**

*Hertz Rent a Car, 1957*

*Howard Johnson's, 1957*

OPENING

SUMMER 1955

*THE SPECTACULAR NEW*

*Beverly Hilton*

BEVERLY HILLS    CALIFORN

ARTHUR E. ELMIGER, *General Manager*

Sheraton Hotels, 1955

Hotel
**Nacional de Cuba**
HAVANA

A Kirkeby Hotel

Hotel Nacional de Cuba, 1953

**This is Florida**—Sunshine, U.S.A.—where everything you do and every place you go are filled with glorious adventure.

This year take it *all* in—the brilliance of Florida's palm-fringed beaches and sun-warmed surf; the tingling excitement of landing that first, or *hundred*-and-first, big-game fish; the thrill of driving one down the middle of velvet-green fairway. This year discover for yourself the splendor of Florida's scenic landmarks; the glamour of its renowned spectator events; the romance of its nights under the stars. And this year see with your own eyes why so many millions agree, there's no place like Florida for sunny pleasure, healthful relaxation, and sheer good living.

***Plan it today**—your sparkling Winter with Sunshine in Florida—the vacation adventure you'll remember a lifetime.

*Florida*

**MAIL THIS COUPON TODAY**

STATE OF FLORIDA,
2201 COMMISSION BUILDING, TALLAHASSEE.

*Please send at once new, free 48-page booklet in full color: "Florida, the Sunshine State."*

Name_____

Street and No._____

City_____Zone___State____

IN CHICAGO IT'S THE
SHERATON
HOTEL

IN BALTIMORE IT'S THE
SHERATON
-BELVEDERE